FRANCES WOODWARD

# Phonics Stories
## for Older Learners

Illustrations by Grant Dudley

**Imprimata**

## forward with p)honics

Phonics Stories for Older Learners
Published by Imprimata
Copyright © Frances Woodward 2012

Illustrations by Grant Dudley.

A CIP Catalogue record for this book is available from the British Library

ISBN 978-1-906192-66-2

Phonics Resources and Phonics Stories for Older Learners
Bundle ISBN 978-1-906192-71-6

Printed in Great Britain

## Imprimata

**An imprint of InXmedia Limited**

*www.imprimata.co.uk*

# Introduction

These stories are graded within a phonic progression, which takes the learner from simple to more complex. They have been written especially for older children, adult and ESOL learners.

They follow the phonic progression that is presented in the Sounds~Write programme and are designed to be used alongside that programme. However, they would be useful for any teacher who wants to introduce the English alphabet code gradually, in a structured sequence.

Being able to read a short text, at the right level, will give the learners confidence and a sense of achievement. It is important to reinforce work on the sounds at each level with reading words in text. Each story includes the sounds taught in that unit and the sounds already learned in previous units, so that the learner can decode every word and gain confidence from independent reading.

The stories are divided into two sections.

**Section One** contains stories which introduce the English alphabet code in its simplest form: single-letter sounds and consonant digraphs, within CVC words in the initial stages. The level of difficulty increases gradually to include 4 and 5 sound words, such as CCCVC. This progression correlates to the Initial Code of the Sounds-Write programme and Phases 2, 3 and 4 of Letters and Sounds.

**Section Two** contains stories that focus on the main vowel phonemes in our language. It correlates to the Extended Code of the Sounds~Write programme and Phases 3 and 5 of Letters and Sounds.

There are two levels in this section:

**Level 1** are simpler stories containing a limited number of graphemes representing the target sound.

**Level 2** are more complex stories and contain more ways of spelling that sound.

Appropriate polysyllabic words are included in each section.

The stories can also be used to consolidate code knowledge. The Sound Search activity, outlined on page 93, helps to enhance aural discrimination by asking the learners to listen for the target sound. Analysing the words containing that sound helps them to identify the various ways of spelling the sound.

A book containing extensive phonic resources suitable for older learners can be ordered from **www.forwardwithphonics.com**

# Phonic Stories
# for Older Learners

# Section One

# Contents - Section One

The pot is on a mat.

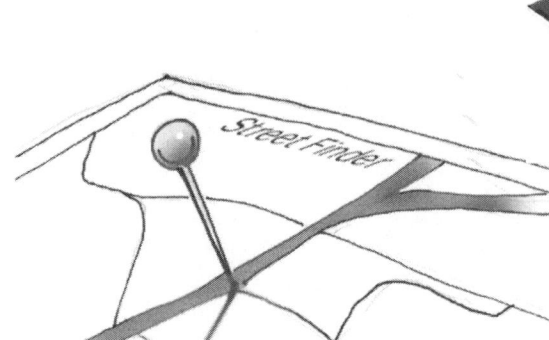

The pin is in a map.

The tin is on the top.

Tip it in a pit.

Tap it in Sam.

Tim sat on a mat.

## Choose a word for each sentence:

| Tap | map | sat | Tip | mat | tin |
|-----|-----|-----|-----|-----|-----|

1. The _____ is on the top.

2. _____ it in Sam.

3. Tim _____ on a mat.

4. The pot is on a _____.

5. _____ it in a pit.

6. The pin is in a _____.

## Fill in the missing letter to make a word from the story:

| m_t | pi_ | _ot | s_t |
|-----|-----|-----|-----|
| to_ | S_m | Ti_ | t_n |

## Copy and read these sentences:

1. The pan is on the top.

_____

2. Sam sat on a pin.

_____

3. Sit on the mat Tom.

_____

The man has a big hat.

The man is hot.

The man got a fan.

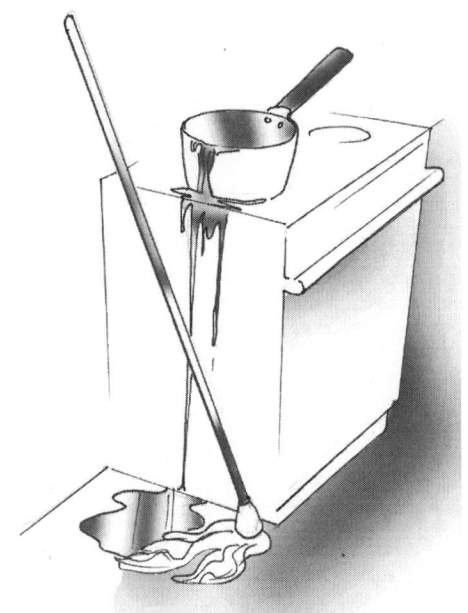

The pan is on the gas.

The pan is hot.

The man got a mop.

The dog is in a van.

The dog is hot.

Is it a hot dog?

## Choose a word for each sentence:

| hot | fan | big | mop | dog | pan |
|-----|-----|-----|-----|-----|-----|

1. The man has a _____ hat.

2. The man got a _____.

3. The _____ is on the gas.

4. The man got a _____.

5. The dog is _____.

6. Is it a hot _____?

## Fill in the missing vowel (a : o : i) to make a word from the story:

| m_n | p_n | d_g | g_s | h_t |
|-----|-----|-----|-----|-----|
| g_t | b_g | f_n | m_p | v_n |

## Read these sentences. Write 'yes' or 'no':

1. The man has a big cat. _____

2. The pan is on the gas. _____

3. The dog is hot. _____

Zac can run.

Zac is fit.

Zac has a red kit.

His dog is not fit.

His dog is fat.

Zac and his dog are hot.

Zac got his fan.

The dog hops on his lap.

Zac and his dog had fun.

## Choose a word for each sentence:

| dog | run | hops | Zac | red | hot |

1. Zac can _____.

2. Zac has a _____ kit.

3. His _____ is not fit.

4. Zac and his dog are _____.

5. _____ got his fan.

6. The dog _____ on his lap.


Find 3 words in the story with \<a> in the middle:

_____    _____    _____

Find 3 words in the story with \<i> in the middle:

_____    _____    _____

Find 3 words in the story with \<o> in the middle:

_____    _____    _____

# Bill's Hut

Bill is in his hut.
It is a mess.
Six mugs, ten pegs,
a rat in a box,
a rod, a net
and a big bag of logs.

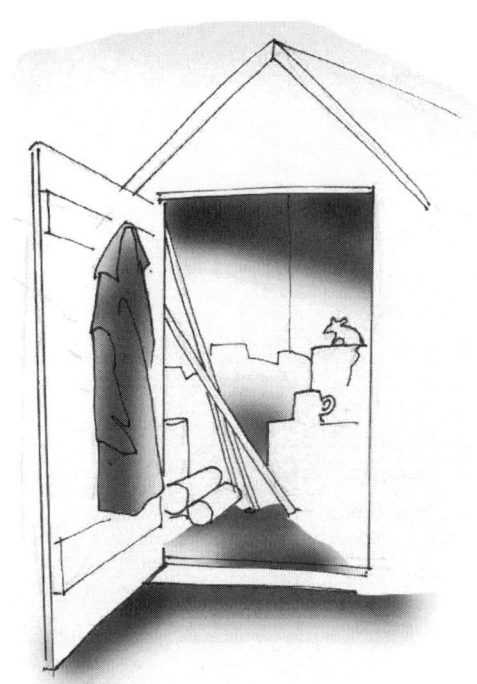

His mac has a rip.
It has mud on the cuff and jam on the zip.

Bill will get rid of the mess.
It will fill ten big boxes.

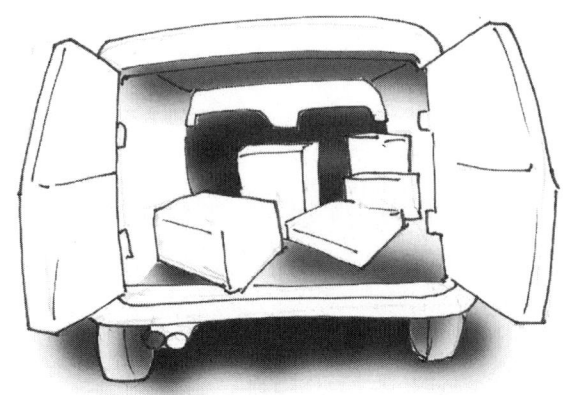

Bill gets the boxes
in his van.
Bill is off to the tip.

## Choose a word for each sentence:

| zip | mac | hut | van | mess | rid |
|-----|-----|-----|-----|------|-----|

1. Bill is in his _____.

2. It is a _____.

3. His _____ has a rip.

4. It has jam on the _____.

5. Bill will get _____ of the mess.

6. Bill gets the boxes in his _____.

Join the words that rhyme (sound the same):
eg. dog ········ fog

| | |
|-----|-----|
| mat | got |
| hot | man |
| big | sat |
| tin | dig |
| pan | sit |
| fit | bin |

Think of a word that rhymes:

six _____　　　　net _____　　　　fill _____

# Rob's Pen

Rob has lost his pen.

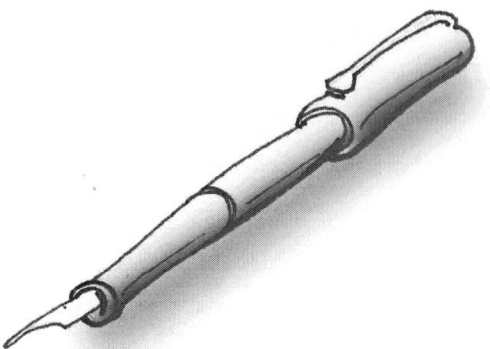

It is not in his bag.
It is not on the desk.

Rob is upset. It is his best pen. It cost a lot.

Bill sent a gift to Rob.
It is a pen.

Rob held the pen in his hand.
It must not get lost.

It can sit on his desk
next to his lamp.

## Choose a word for each sentence:

| gift | upset | lost | held | lamp | cost |
|------|-------|------|------|------|------|

1. Rob has _____ his pen.

2. Rob is _____.

3. The pen _____ a lot.

4. Bill sent Rob a _____.

5. Rob _____ the pen in his hand.

6. The pen is next to the _____.

## Fill in the missing vowel (a, e, i, o, u) to make a word from the story:

| l_st | d_sk | b_st | c_st | s_nt |
|------|------|------|------|------|
| g_ft | h_ld | h_nd | m_st | l_mp |

## Choose 3 words from the box and write a sentence for each:

_____  _____

_____  _____

_____  _____

_____  _____

_____  _____

_____  _____

# The Flat

Fred and Scott are twins.

Fred and Scott live in a flat.
The flat is a mess. It has a bad smell.

Lots of pots are in the sink.
The tap drips.
The grill is in bits.

Fred and Scott plan to get rid of the mess.
Fred will stop the drip.
Scott will fix the grill.

Fred and Scott are glad to get rid of the bad smell.

## Choose a word for each sentence:

| flat | sink | mend | grill | twins | bad |
|------|------|------|-------|-------|-----|

1. Fred and Scott are _____.

2. They live in a _____.

3. The flat has a _____ smell.

4. There are pots in the _____.

5. The _____ is in bits.

6. Fred will _____ the drip.

## Fill in the missing vowel (a, e, i, o, u) to make a word from the story:

| tw_n | fl_t | sm_ll | s_nk | dr_p |
|------|------|-------|------|------|
| gr_ll | m_ss | pl_n | st_p | gl_d |

## Write these sentences with capital letters and full stops:

1. fred and scott are twins

_____

2. the flat is a mess

_____

3. scott will fix the grill

_____

# The Crisps

Frank sits on the steps. Frank gets a big bag of crisps from his bag.

His dog, Scrap, smells the crisps.
Scrap jumps up.

Scrap grabs the crisps and runs off.

Frank stands up and yells at Scrap.
Frank is cross. The crisps cost a lot.

Scrap drops the crisps on the wet sand.
The bag splits.

The gulls get the crisps and Scrap is cross. Frank is cross too.

## Choose a word for each sentence:

| drops   jumps   cross   steps   Scrap   splits |
|---|

1. Frank sits on the _____.

2. Scrap _____ up.

3. Frank yells at _____.

4. Scrap _____ the crisps.

5. The bag _____.

6. Scrap is _____.

## Join the words that rhyme:

bag           band

sit            drag

smell        lost

stand       stop

drop        split

cost        tell

## Think of a word that rhymes:

drill _____          send _____          pink _____

# At the Shops

Trish and Josh went on a trip
to the shops.

Trish got a dish, a brush
and cash from the bank.

Josh got a drill, a shelf
and a pink shrub in a pot.

They had to dash from shop to shop.
It was a rush.

Did they finish?
Yes – just as
the shops shut at six.

## Choose a word for each sentence:

| dash    shops    shut    shrub    rush    cash |

1. Trish and Josh went to the _____.

2. Trish got _____ from the bank.

3. Josh got a pink _____ in a pot.

4. They had to _____ from shop to shop.

5. It was a _____ .

6. The shops _____ at six.

## Add <sh> to these words:

| __ops        di__        bru__        ca__ |
| ru__        __elf        __rub        __ut |

## Choose 3 words from the box and write a sentence for each:

_____    _____

            _____

_____    _____

            _____

_____    _____

            _____

# Chips for Lunch

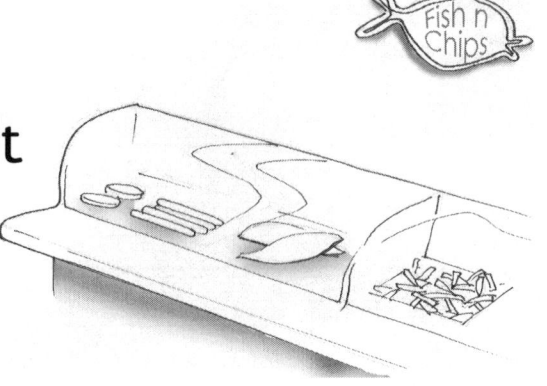

It was 1.30pm.
Chaz, Jill and Rich went
to the chip shop
for lunch.

Jill had chicken and chips.
Chaz had fish and chips.
Rich had a big bag of chips and got
ketchup on his chin.

Chaz got a text from Prem – 'lunch? x'
Chaz sent a text back
– 'cum 2 chip shop. x'

Prem sat on the bench
and had a chip sandwich.
They all had a can of drink.

What a mess !

## Choose a word for each sentence:

| text   drink   ketchup   chicken   bench   chips |
| --- |

1. Jill had _____ and chips.

2. Chaz had fish and _____.

3. Rich got _____ on his chin.

4. Chaz got a _____ from Prem.

5. Prem sat on the _____.

6. They all had a can of _____.

## Add <ch> to these words:

| __az | __ip | lun__ | ket__up |
| --- | --- | --- | --- |
| ben__ | __in | __icken | sandwi__ |

## Choose 3 words from the box and write a sentence for each:

_____   _____

_____

_____   _____

_____

_____   _____

_____

# The Swim

Beth went for a swim with Brad.
Beth can swim well.
Beth swims to the end.
The depth is 3.5m.
Brad swims a width.
That was not bad for him.

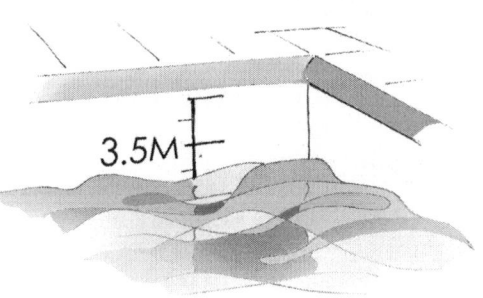

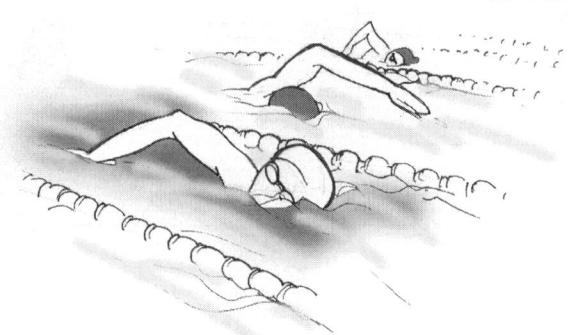

They swim with the children. Brad thinks
that they can swim well.
They swim fast.
Beth is fifth
but Brad is last.

Beth had to help Brad get to the end.
"Thanks Beth. Let's go and get dressed."

Then they went for a
hot drink with the
children.

## Choose a word for each sentence:

| fifth   width   children   drink   swim   dressed |
|---|

1. Beth went for a _____ with Brad.

2. Brad swims a _____ .

3. They swim with the _____ .

4. Beth is _____ but Brad is last.

5. Let's go and get _____ .

6. They went for a hot _____ .

## Add <th> to these words:

| Be___ | wid___ | ___at | ___ey |
|---|---|---|---|
| ___ink | fif___ | ___ank | ___en |

## Choose 3 words from the box and write a sentence for each:

_____  _____

_____

_____  _____

_____

_____  _____

_____

# The Duck

Jack went to check his chickens.
Jack has ten chickens
and six chicks.
One egg has not hatched yet.
The hen will sit on the egg till it cracks.

There is a sack in the shed.
The chicks peck at
the sack.

A duck comes up from the pond. It sticks
its neck into the shed.
The duck is in luck.
The sack rips.
The duck quacks at the
chicks.
The chicks run.

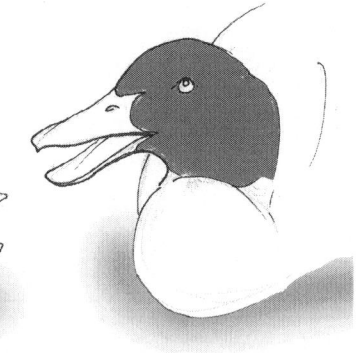

The duck has his fill and skulks back to
the pond.

## Choose a word for each sentence:

| chicks | egg | duck | ten | shed | peck |
|---|---|---|---|---|---|

1. Jack has _____ chickens.

2. The hen will sit on the _____.

3. The chicks _____ at the sack.

4. A _____ comes up from the pond.

5. It sticks its neck in the _____.

6. The duck quacks at the _____.

## Add <ck> to these words:

| che___ | chi___ | cra___ | sa___ |
|---|---|---|---|
| pe___ | sti___ | qua___ | du___ |

## Choose 3 words from the box and write a sentence for each:

_____  _____

        _____

_____  _____

        _____

_____  _____

        _____

# The Visit

Gran is not well.
Mum and the children visit
Gran and bring the shopping.

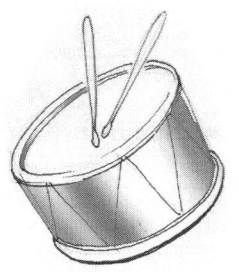

Jen has a drum
and bangs it with a stick.

Beth has a doll that
can sing a song.

Max has a truck which
clanks along a track.

"What a din," yells Gran
from under the quilt.

"Quick" says Mum,
"Let's get back to get Dad his lunch."
"Thanks," said Gran. "Can you let the
children go to the swings when you visit
next time?"

## Choose a word for each sentence:

| truck    well    swings    drum    quilt    doll |
|---|

1. Gran is not _____.

2. Jen bangs the _____ with a stick.

3. Beth has a _____.

4. The _____ clanks along a track.

5. Gran is under the _____.

6. Can the children go to the _____ next time?

## Join the words that rhyme:

| well | bunch |
|---|---|
| bring | text |
| stick | sack |
| track | bell |
| lunch | sing |
| next | brick |

## Think of a word that rhymes:

hand _____          wish _____          chip _____

# Phonic Stories
# for Older Learners

# Section Two

# Section Two

This section is divided into two levels:

**Level 1**

These stories are for those learners who are learning to read for the first time and have a limited knowledge of the alphabet code. They contain a limited number of graphemes for each of the target sounds. They are simple in structure and are in larger print. This makes them easier to read for a beginner reader and easier to see if projected onto an Interactive Whiteboard for group reading. This level corresponds to the 'First Spellings' section in the Extended Code of the Sounds~Write programme and Phases 3 and 5 of Letters and Sounds.

**Level 2**

These stories are for use at a later date, when the learner has completed Level 1 and has a good understanding of the code, or for more able learners. They are more challenging; contain more polysyllabic words and the full range of the graphemes that represent the target sounds. This corresponds to the 'More Spellings' section in the Extended Code of the Sounds~Write programme and Phases 3 and 5 of Letters and Sounds.

# Contents - Section Two

## Level 1

## Level 2

# Section Two
## Level 1

# Jane and Jake

Jane went to the shops on the train.
The train was late and Jane had to wait in the rain.

Jane met Jake at the shops.

Jake had a pot of paint and nails to mend his gate.
Jane got a red dress to take on holiday to Spain.
They got milk shakes and cake on a tray.

They sat and had a long chat.
They had a great day.

Find the missing word in the story:

1. Jane went to the shops on the _____.

2. Jane had to _____ in the rain.

3. Jane met _____ at the shops.

4. Jake had a pot of paint and _____ to mend his gate.

5. Jane got a _____ dress.

6. They got milk shakes and _____ on a tray.

7. They had a long _____.

8. They had a _____ day.


Find 3 words in the story containing the sound 'ae':

_____          _____          _____


Write a sentence for each word:

_____

_____

_____

_____

_____

# Pete's Jeep

The jeep went up
a steep hill.
It hit a rock and
a wheel came off.
Pete sat on a seat near a field of sheep.

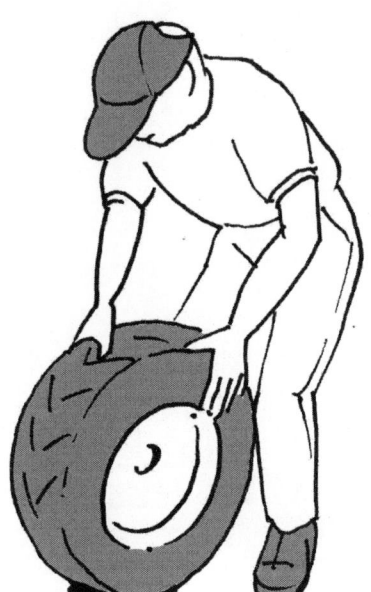

He was very happy
to see a man come up
the hill. He had a wheel
for the jeep.

It was three o'clock
when Pete got back.
He had a cup of tea
and a sticky cream bun.

"What a week this has been," said Pete.

Find the missing word in the story:

1. The jeep went up a _____ hill.

2. A _____ came off.

3. Pete sat on a _____.

4. The field had _____ in it.

5. The man came up the _____.

6. He had a _____ for the jeep.

7. It was _____ when Pete got back.

8. He had a cup of _____ and a _____ cream bun.

Find a word in the story for each spelling of 'ee':

\<ee\>_____          \<ea\>_____

\<ie\> _____          \<y\> _____

Write a sentence for each word:

_____

_____

_____

_____

_____

_____

# Joe Gets Post

Joe woke up.
He went to the window.
"It is cold today.
I think it will snow."

Joe got his thick coat and
went up the road.
Joe met the postman.
He gave Joe his post.

It was a note from his old mate Tony.
So Joe went home to read his note.

Then he made himself
a cup of tea
and loads of toast.

# Find the missing word in the story:

1. Joe went to the _____.

2. Joe thinks it will _____.

3. Joe got his _____ coat.

4. He met the _____.

5. Joe got a _____ from his old mate Tony.

6. He went _____ to read his note.

7. Joe made himself a cup of _____.

8. He had _____ of toast.

Underline the spelling for 'oe' in these words:

| Joe | cold | coat | note | home | toast |

Choose 3 words from the box and write a sentence for each:

_____

_____

_____

_____

# Lunch with Curtis

Every Thursday Verna
meets Curtis for lunch.

Last Thursday she left
work early. She went to
the shops first.
Then she met Curtis
and they had burger
and chips.

It got late. Verna had
to hurry back to work.
As she went to cross
over the road she fell
and everything in her bag spilt all over
the road. She felt very silly. She hurt her
leg and her skirt got dirty.

Curtis helped her up.
"Thanks Curtis. I must rush.
See you later."

Find the missing word in the story:

1. Every _____ Verna meets Curtis for lunch.

2. Last week she left work _____.

3. She went to the _____ first.

4. They had _____ and chips.

5. _____ had to hurry back to work.

6. Everything in her bag spilt all over the _____.

7. Her _____ got dirty.

8. _____ helped her up.


Find 3 words in the story containing the sound 'er':

_____        _____        _____


Write a sentence for each word:

_____

_____

_____

_____

_____

# Bread

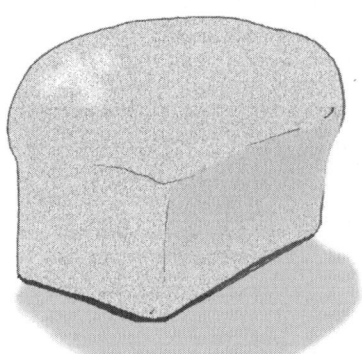

Fred can eat bread
at any time.

He has it for breakfast
with bacon.

He has it for lunch with egg.

He has it for tea
with jam.

His friend Ben said "Bread tends to make
you fat."

"Then I will get very heavy." said Fred.

## Find the missing word in the story:

1. Fred can eat _____ at any time.

2. He has it for _____ with bacon.

3. He has it for lunch with _____ .

4. He has it for _____ with jam.

5. Fred's friend is _____ .

6. He said, "Bread tends to make you _____ ."

7. "Then I will get very _____ ," said Fred.


## Find 3 words in the story containing the sound 'e':

_____          _____          _____


## Write a sentence for each word:

_____

_____

_____

_____

_____

# Out of Town

We drove out of town.
We found a field
for a picnic
and sat down on the
ground to have our lunch.

The day was hot and
sunny with no clouds.
The only sound was a
mouse squeaking as
it hid from the brown
owl up in the tree.

Then a crowd came out
of the old house.
They began to run
around and shout.

How sad. We had to pack
up our picnic and go back to town.

## Find the missing word in the story:

1. We drove out of _____.

2. We _____ a field for a picnic.

3. We sat on the _____ to have our lunch.

4. The day was hot and _____.

5. The only sound was a mouse _____.

6. The brown _____ was up in the tree.

7. A crowd came out of the _____ house.

8. We went back to _____.

## Underline the spelling for 'ow' in these words:

| out | town | ground | cloud | mouse | crowd |

## Choose 3 words from the box and write a sentence for each:

_____

_____

_____

_____

# The Blue Boots

Sue and Lou went to the
shoe shop.
"Do you want black
boots?" asked Lou.
"No, I need blue boots
to go with the blue suit."
"That is true," said Lou,
who always agreed with Sue.

At the back of the
shoe shop was a room,
where they sold food.
Sue had a fruit juice
and Lou had soup.

In June, Sue threw out her old boots.
Now she has blue boots to go with her
blue suit.

Find the missing word in the story:

1. Sue and Lou went to the _____ shop.

2. "Do you want _____ boots?" asked Lou.

3. "I need _____ boots," said Sue.

4. Lou always _____ with Sue.

5. At the back of the shop was a _____.

6. Sue had _____ _____ and Lou had soup.

7. In _____ Sue threw out her old boots.

8. She has _____ boots to go with her
    _____ suit.

Find a word in the story for each spelling of 'oo':

<oo>_____          <ue>_____

<ui> _____          <ou>_____

Write a sentence for each word:

_____

_____

_____

_____

_____

# Mike's Ride

Friday is Mike's day off.
He goes for a ride on
his bike. He cycles to
the top of a high hill.

He feels tired, so
has a lie down in
the sunshine.

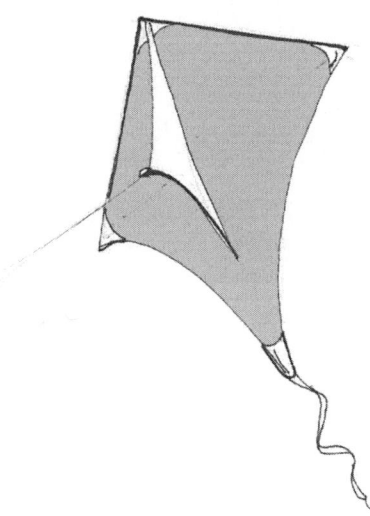

Mike sees five children flying
kites in the field near by.
The kites fly high in the sky.

Mike thinks he might like to
try that one day.

Soon it is nine o'clock.
It is  time for Mike to
ride home.

## Find the missing word in the story:

1. _____ is Mike's day off.

2. He goes for a _____ on his bike.

3. He cycles up a high _____.

4. Mike lies down in the _____.

5. Mike sees _____ children.

6. The kites fly high in the _____.

7. Soon it is _____ o'clock.

8. Mike rides _____.

## Underline the spelling for 'ie' in these words:

| Friday | ride | high | lie | sky | might |

Choose 3 words from the box and write a sentence for each one:

_____

_____

_____

_____

# The Crook

The crook hid in the bush.
He had a bag full of
stolen goods.

He pulled up his hood
and took the path
into the woods.

He should run.
They would look for
him in the woods.

If only he could reach the road he would
be safe.

He put his bag
under a bush.
He would come back
for it later.

Find the missing word in the story:

1. The _____ hid in the bush.

2. His bag was full of _____ goods.

3. He pulled up his _____.

4. He took the _____ into the woods.

5. He _____ run.

6. He would be safe if he could reach the _____.

7. He put his _____ under a bush.

8. He would come back for it _____.

Find 3 words in the story containing the sound 'oo':

_____          _____          _____

Write a sentence for each word:

_____

_____

_____

_____

_____

# The Storm

Last August there was an awful storm.
Paul and I were out
in it for hours.

We had gone for
a walk to see the
horses on the moor.

Then we saw the
storm clouds.
It began to rain
and the wind was
strong.

It tore up the small trees and all the
straw for the horses had blown about.

We crawled into a hole in a wall for
shelter. I will always remember that day.

Find the missing word in the story:

1. Last _____ there was an awful storm.

2. We were _____ in it for hours.

3. We had gone to see the _____ on the moor.

4. Then we saw the storm _____.

5. The _____ was strong.

6. It tore up the small _____.

7. The _____ for the horses had blown about.

8. We crawled into a hole for _____.

Find 3 words in the story containing the sound 'or':

_____        _____        _____

Write a sentence for each word:

_____

_____

_____

_____

# The Hairdresser

Clare went to the hairdressers. She was scared he would cut it too short.
She sat in the chair to wait.

"Where are my scissors?" shouted Anton.
"I've looked everywhere".
"You can share mine," offered Dan.
"I'll get a spare pair," said Anton.

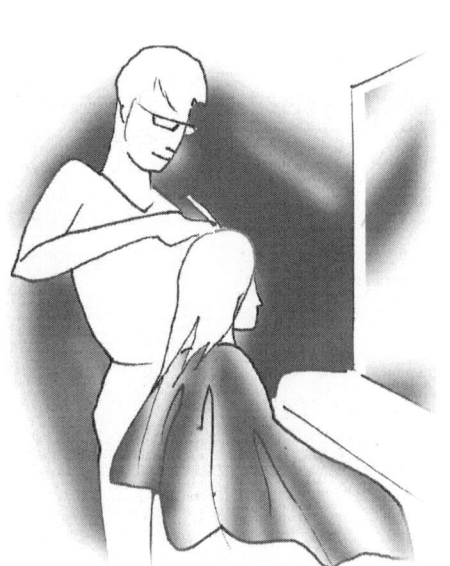

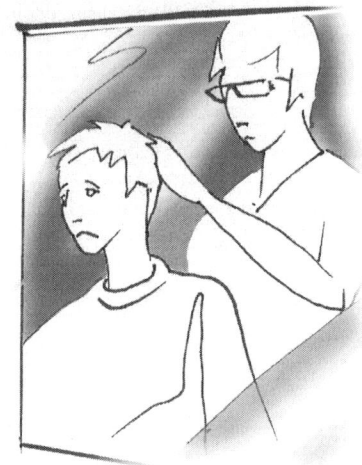

At last he began to cut Clare's hair.
He cut and cut and cut.
Clare stared in the mirror.
"There," said Anton, unaware of her despair.
Clare left the shop and went off to get a hat to wear!

Find the missing word in the story:

1. Clare went to the _____.

2. She sat in the _____ to wait.

3. "Where are my _____?" shouted Anton.

4. "You can _____ mine," offered Dan.

5. "I'll get a spare _____," said Anton.

6. He began to _____ Clare's hair.

7. Clare _____ in the mirror.

8. Clare went off to get a _____ to wear.

Underline the spelling for 'air' in these words:

| Clare | chair | where | share | pair | wear |
|-------|-------|-------|-------|------|------|

Choose 3 words from the box and write a
sentence for each one:

_____

_____

_____

_____

# On the Farm

Karl is a farmer. He gets up at half past six to milk the cows.

His dog, Arthur, helps him with the sheep.
He runs fast.
Karl stays calm as Arthur follows his commands.

The children help their father. They clean out the barn and sweep the yard.

His wife looks after the farm shop.
On Fridays she goes to market.

It is hard work living on a farm.

Find the missing word in the story:

1. Karl is a _____.

2. He gets up at _____ _____ _____.

3. _____ helps him with the sheep.

4. Arthur _____ his commands.

5. The children help their _____.

6. They clean out the _____.

7. Karl's wife looks after the farm _____.

8. On _____ she goes to market.

Find a word in the story for each spelling of 'ar':

<ar>_____          <al>_____

<a> _____

Write a sentence for each word:

_____

_____

_____

_____

_____

# Section Two
## Level 2

# Off to Spain

Mr and Mrs Grey go on holiday to Spain every year.

They pack their cases and set off for the railway station. They wait for ages for the train to take them to the airport. Mr Grey looks at the timetable.

"Oh no! I have made a mistake. They changed the times of the trains at the end of April. Today is the eighth of May!"

Mrs Grey is not pleased.
They have to wait for the next train. It makes them very late. They nearly miss their plane.

"All passengers for mainland Spain please make your way to Gate Eighteen. We're afraid there will be a slight delay because of this heavy rain."

"Great," said Mrs Grey. We have made it! Let's hope there is no rain in Spain. I want to sit in the shade and read the paper all day!"

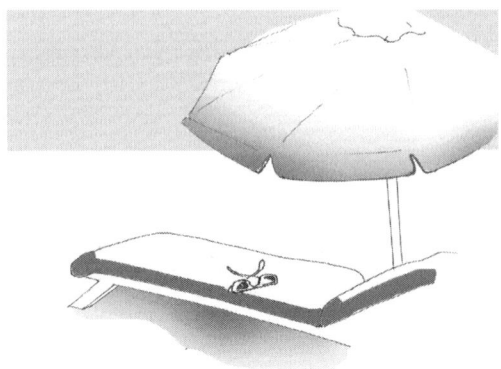

"I can't wait", said Mr Grey.

# Write your answers in sentences:

1. Who went to Spain every year?

_____

2. How did they get to the airport?

_____

3. What happened at the end of April?

_____

4. On what date did they travel?

_____

5. Why was Mrs Grey cross?

_____

6. What gate number did they go to?

_____

7. Why was the plane delayed?

_____

8. What did Mrs Grey want to do in Spain?

_____

Write 3-4 sentences about a holiday or day out:

_____

_____

_____

_____

# A Birthday Treat

Peter took his family out for a meal to celebrate his wife Jean's birthday.

"What would you like to eat Jean? It's my treat."

Jean decided to have the leek soup to start. Then she had beef in gravy with beans and potatoes.

Peter had pea soup and then his favourite chicken curry. Josie, their daughter, had veal with roast potatoes and peas.

For dessert they all had cheesecake followed by coffee with cream.

"That was delicious", said Jean at the end of the evening. Thank you. Let's take a taxi home. That will be my treat!"

# Write your answers in sentences:

1. Why did Peter take his family out for a meal?

_____

2. What soup did Jean have?

_____

3. What did Jean have next?

_____

4. What soup did Peter have?

_____

5. What did Peter have next?

_____

6. What sort of potatoes did Josie have?

_____

7. What did they all have to drink?

_____

8. How did they get home?

_____

Find 4 words in the story containing the sound 'ee':

_____     _____     _____     _____

Write a sentence for each word:

_____

_____

_____

_____

_____

# Snow in October

One morning in late October, Joe was woken by the phone ringing next to his bed. His sister, Joan, spoke very quickly. She sounded excited. "Joe! Go and look out of the window."
"What for?" moaned Joe. "I want to go back to sleep."

"Just go and look, Joe. It's snowing!"

Joe got up slowly. It was cold and he wanted to stay in his warm bed. Joe looked out and saw the snow.

The children from next door had built a snowman in the garden. He had big stones for his eyes, small stones for his mouth and a carrot for a nose. He had an old hat on his head.

Joe put on his thick coat and opened the back door. It was great to make footprints in the fresh snow.

He went up the road and met Tony, the postman. "Hello, Joe. What a surprise to get snow in October! Here's your post."

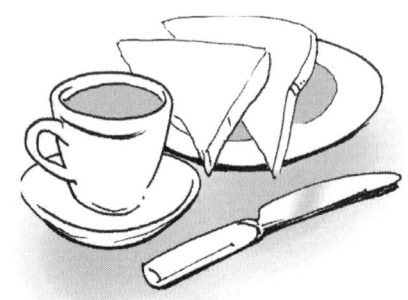

Joe took his letters home and made himself some tea and toast.

# Write your answers in sentences:

1. What woke Joe up?

_____

2. What did Joan tell Joe to do?

_____

3. What was the weather like that morning?

_____

4. What did Joe see in the garden next door?

_____

5. What did the snowman have on his head?

_____

6. What did Joe like doing in the fresh snow?

_____

7. Who did Joe meet?

_____

8. What did Joe have when he got home?

_____

Underline the spellings for the sound 'oe' in these words:

| Joe | Joan | spoke | window | snow |
|-----|------|-------|--------|------|
| old | coat | toast | stones | post |

Choose 4 words from the box and write a sentence for each one:

_____

_____

_____

_____

_____

# Nurse Turner

Nurse Turner rushed into work at thirteen minutes past eight. Her shift started at eight but she had overslept. She worked at Manchester Royal Infirmary in the centre of the city. The traffic was worse than usual this morning.

"Quick," said her friend, Kirsty. " Sister is coming to inspect the ward at eight-thirty."

"That's the first I've heard of it," said Nurse Turner. "I'd better go and get a clean uniform. This collar is dirty and my skirt is too short. Sister likes everything to be perfect."

After the inspection, Sister turned to Nurse Turner. "I've heard a rumour that you are often late for work. Make sure you are early next Thursday. We have a new doctor starting and I want to be certain that we are all here to welcome her."

Nurse Turner smiled as she got on with her work. She had got away with her bad start to the day.

She was determined not to be late on Thursday. She would be early to impress the new doctor!

# Write your answers in sentences:

1. What time did Nurse Turner get to work?

_____

2. Where did she work?

_____

3. Why was she late for work?

_____

4. What was happening at 8.30am?

_____

5. Why did she have to get a clean uniform?

_____

6. What word means 'as good as it can be'?

_____

7. What day is the new doctor starting?

_____

8. Why was Nurse Turner determined to be early?

_____

Write 3-4 sentences about a trip to hospital:

_____

_____

_____

_____

_____

# Eggs for Breakfast

Ben and Ed are friends. They share a flat above a chip shop. Ben likes to keep fit. He wants to run in the London Marathon next year. He goes to the gym three times a week and goes for a run every morning before work. Ed is meant to go with him but he never gets up in time.

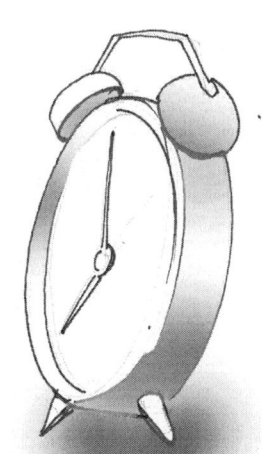

Last Sunday Ben's alarm went off at 7am. He leapt out of bed and put on his shorts and the new T shirt his mum had bought him. It had 'Ready, Steady, Go!' on the front. He wore a head band and sweat bands on his wrists. It was a lovely morning. He ran for ten miles.

When he got back to the flat, Ed was cooking breakfast. "Do you want any breakfast Ben?" asked Ed. "I'm having

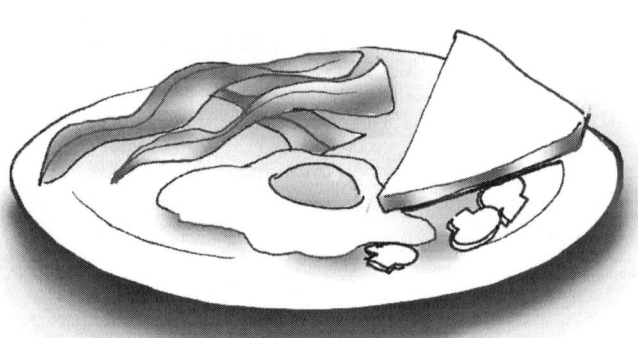

egg, bacon, sausage, tomatoes and mushrooms."
"That doesn't sound very healthy," said Ben, "If I ate all that I would be too heavy to run! I'll just have eggs, thanks."

"How many eggs then?" asked Ed.
"Can you do me two eggs on some bread? That might give me the energy to go for a shower!"

# Write your answers in sentences:

1. Where do Ben and Ed live?

_____

2. What race does Ben want to run next year?

_____

3. How often does he go to the gym?

_____

4. What time did Ben get up last Sunday?

_____

5. What was printed on Ben's T shirt?

_____

6. How far did Ben run?

_____

7. What was Ed having for breakfast?

_____

8. What did Ben have for breakfast?

_____


What do you like for breakfast?

_____

_____

_____


How do you keep fit?

_____

_____

_____

# Mouse in the House

Mrs Brown sat in the lounge watching TV. Mr Brown was in the garden reading his book. It was a cloudy day but still very warm. Suddenly, he heard a shout from inside the house. Mrs Brown came running out.

"There's a mouse, there's a mouse!" she screamed loudly.
"Calm down," said Mr Brown. "Where is this mouse?"
"It's under the couch in the lounge. I'm staying outside now."

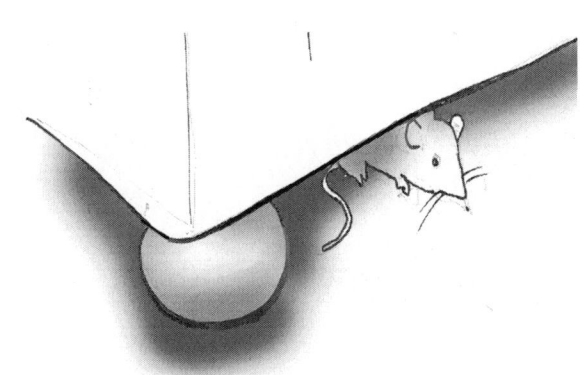

Mr Brown went into the lounge and chased the mouse out of the house. "You are such a coward. It is only a little brown mouse. You have frightened it with all your shouting!

Look he is crouching on the ground under the flowers.

I don't think he will come into our house again!"

# Write your answers in sentences:

1. What was Mrs Brown doing?

_____

2. What was Mr Brown doing?

_____

3. Why did Mrs Brown scream?

_____

4. Where was the mouse?

_____

5. What colour was the mouse?

_____

6. What did Mr Brown do?

_____

7. Where did the mouse go?

_____

8. Why would the mouse probably not come back?

_____

Find 4 words in the story containing the sound 'ow':

_____     _____     _____     _____

Write a sentence for each word:

_____

_____

_____

_____

_____

# The Cruise

Sue and Bruce were looking forward to their holiday. They were going on a cruise around the Greek Islands.

On June 6th they flew to Athens and were soon boarding the big ship that was to be their home for the next two weeks.

"Our room is number forty-two," said Sue.
"I think you mean cabin," laughed Bruce. "Look, it is the one with the blue door."

Inside was very big. There were four bedrooms, a sitting room and two bathrooms. "This is too big for us," said Bruce. "Look, there are shoes under the bed and a suit in the wardrobe. There's toothpaste and shampoo in the bathroom." Just then there was a knock at the door.

"I'm sorry," said the steward, "There has been a mistake. This is for a group of people who all want to be together. Do you mind moving to number two hundred and two? I will take your cases, just follow me."

Having to move did not ruin their holiday. Number two hundred and two was smaller and suited them much better.

The route took them to some beautiful islands and some secluded beaches.

The crew were all very helpful and the food was delicious.

It was the best holiday they had ever had.

# Write your answers in sentences:

1. Where were Sue and Bruce going on holiday?

_____

2. On what date did they go?

_____

3. What is a room on a ship called?

_____

4. How many bedrooms did cabin 42 have?

_____

5. What was under the bed?

_____

6. What number cabin did they move to?

_____

7. What does the word 'secluded' mean?

_____

8. How did Sue and Bruce describe their holiday?

_____

Underline the spellings for the sound 'oo' in these words:

| Sue | cruise | June | soon | blue |
|-----|--------|------|------|------|
| shoe | room | move | group | crew |

Choose 4 words from the box and write a sentence for each one:

_____

_____

_____

_____

_____

# A Healthy Diet

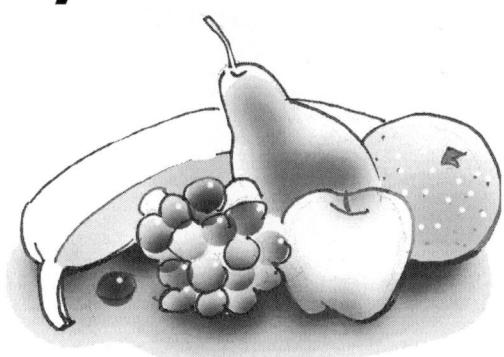

We all know the importance of a healthy diet. The number of people that are diagnosed with food related illnesses, such as obesity and diabetes, has increased by 40% in the last nine years.

Everyone knows that high levels of sugar are not good for us but did you know that some foods now contain twice as much sugar as they did thirty years ago!

Even foods, such as soup and breakfast cereals, that you think are healthy, might contain the same amount of sugar that you find in ice-cream.

Last night, at the 'Health and Diet' Conference in China, Mike Fry said, "We need to follow the Government guidelines and eat five helpings of fruit and vegetables each day.

Too many children rely on junk food, which is high in sugar and fat, leading to problems in later life. It is vital that every child, whatever shape or size, is made to realise the importance of exercise and a healthy diet."

The message to our children should be:

## Exercise!!

### "Don't lie on the couch eating pies!

### Get on your bike and ride!"

# Write your answers in sentences:

1. Name two food related illnesses.

_____

2. High levels of what are not good for us?

_____

3. What two foods may contain a lot of sugar?

_____

4. Where was the Health and Diet Conference?

_____

5. What are the Government Guidelines for a healthy diet?

_____

6. What sort of food do a lot of children like?

_____

7. What is bad about junk food?

_____

8. What should we encourage children to do?

_____


Find 4 words in the story containing the sound 'ie':

_____   _____   _____   _____


Write a sentence for each word:

_____

_____

_____

_____

_____

# The Pudding

Last Sunday, it was my best friend's birthday. I invited her to our house for dinner. I decided to make her favourite meal — chicken and roast vegetables.

"Should I make a pudding?" I asked my family.
"That would be good," said the children.
"I could help you," said my husband.

He took the cook book down from the shelf. "Look at this one," he said. "It's called Chocolate Challenge! I could make that."

Into the bowl went the butter, sugar and flour, eggs and milk and lots and lots of chocolate! He mixed it well and poured it into an oven-proof dish. He put it into the oven to cook. It smelt good.

That night, we all enjoyed the dinner.
My friend loved the vegetables and asked for more.

"Sorry, Dad, we're too full for pudding," said the children.
"I couldn't eat another thing," said my friend.

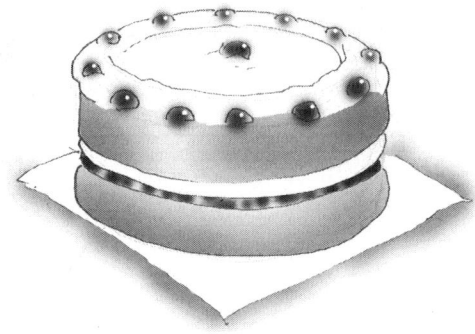

"We could put it in the fridge for tomorrow," I suggested.

"Or — I could eat it all myself," said my husband. " That would be a real Chocolate Challenge!"

# Write your answers in sentences:

1. When was the friend's birthday?

_____

2. What was her favourite meal?

_____

3. Who made the pudding?

_____

4. What was the pudding called?

_____

5. What was in the pudding?

_____

6. How was the pudding cooked?

_____

7. Why couldn't anyone eat the pudding?

_____

8. What did the husband suggest?

_____

Underline the spellings for the sound 'oo' in these words:

| should | pudding | good | could | took |
|--------|---------|------|-------|------|
| would | couldn't | cook | sugar | put |

Choose 4 words from the box and write a sentence for each one:

_____

_____

_____

_____

_____

# Sports Report

# Walker Saves the Day

*4-1 VICTORY puts town on course for the title in their first season*

The game started slowly. Boardsley crawled around the Portsmouth defence and Paul West kicked the ball from the edge of the box, but the goalkeeper dived and caught it.

At half time the score was 1-0 to Portsmouth. Jack Walker was brought on and the pace of the match changed. He scored in the first few minutes and the crowd roared as he ran towards them doing his famous "fall and roll" routine. Boardsley were now fired up. West scored next with excellent support from the forwards. Harry Shaw broke free but was tackled by the Portsmouth defender and fell awkwardly on his right leg. A doctor was called on and Shaw was taken off on a stretcher.

One man down and fourteen minutes to go. Walker scored two fantastic goals and then one more in injury time. Awesome play by the Boardsley striker.

A victory for Boardsley!

The final score :

**Boardsley - 4     Portsmouth - 1**

# Write your answers in sentences:

1. What two teams were playing in the football match?

_____

2. Did Paul West score a goal?

_____

3. What was the score at half time?

_____

4. Which player was brought on in the second half?

_____

5. What was his victory routine called?

_____

6. Which player was injured?

_____

7. What happened to him?

_____

8. How many goals did Walker score?

_____


Write 3-4 sentences about your favourite sport:

_____

_____

_____

_____

_____

# Clare's Nightmare

Clare and Alistair went to see the film, 'Horror at the Funfair'. They bought a drink and some popcorn to share. The film was very scary. Clare hung onto Alistair and covered her face with her hair.

That night Clare had an awful nightmare. She was at the fair with Alistair and they went into the Haunted House. It said, "BEWARE... ENTER IF YOU DARE!"

It was very dark in there and the air was filled with nasty smells and scary noises.

There was a pair of bright green eyes glaring at them. Ghosts floated in the air and a skeleton crept down the stairs. They travelled through cobwebs and a spider got caught in Clare's hair. She screamed and jumped out of the chair. She ran through wet grass. The air was cold.

Someone was shaking her. She opened her eyes and stared. Where was she? She was not at the fair. She was bare foot and wearing her pyjamas!

It had just been a scary nightmare...

# Write your answers in sentences:

1. What film did Clare and Alistair go to see?

_____

2. What happened to Clare that night?

_____

3. What did the sign say outside The Haunted House?

_____

4. What colour were the eyes staring at them?

_____

5. Where did they see a skeleton?

_____

6. What got caught in Clare's hair?

_____

7. What did she do?

_____

8. What was Clare wearing when she woke up?

_____

Find 4 words in the story containing the sound 'air':

_____   _____   _____   _____

Write a sentence for each word:

_____

_____

_____

_____

_____

# The Party

Last Saturday night Maz and Charlie went to a party. They took a long time to get ready and looked very smart in their best clothes.

They set off in Charlie's old car but they were only half way there when it broke down. Charlie was very angry and started to kick the car.

"I'm fed up with this stupid car. It's always breaking down. Now we're going to miss the party!" "Calm down," said Maz. "It won't harm us to walk. It's not far to Carly's house if we go across the park."

So they left the car in a side-road and took the path across the park. They eventually got to the party looking a bit hot and sweaty and not quite as smart as they did when they set out!

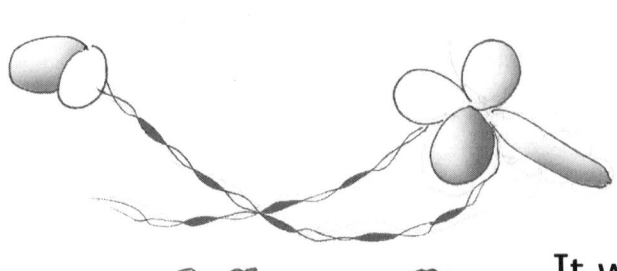

Carly was pleased to see them. They had a laugh with their friends and even asked some girls to dance.

It was after midnight when the party finished and they were the last to leave!

# Write your answers in sentences:

1. On what day did Maz and Charlie go to the party?

_____

2. What happened to the car?

_____

3. How did they get to the party?

_____

4. Where did they leave the car?

_____

5. How did they feel when they got to the party?

_____

6. Was Carly pleased to see them?

_____

7. What did they do at the party?

_____

8. What time did the party finish?

_____


Write 3-4 sentences about a party you have been to:

_____

_____

_____

_____

_____

# Sound Search

This activity is similar to 'Seek the Sound' in the Extended Code section of the Sounds-Write programme and 'Phoneme Spotter' in Phase 5 of Letters and Sounds.

1. Read the story to the learners. This enables them to concentrate on the meaning of the text. The learners can follow the text as you read or just listen.

2. Read the story again, very slowly. Ask the learners to listen and repeat the word if they hear the target sound, eg 'snow', if the target sound is 'oe'. Highlight or underline these words. The learners can do this on their own copy of the story as you progress through the story. However, many find it difficult to listen for the sound and follow the text simultaneously. They can also be distracted by the visual cues, eg. 'hot' does not contain the sound 'oe'. You may prefer to ask them to turn their text over and concentrate on listening for the target sound. You would highlight the words, as they identify them, on your copy of the story.

3. If you have an interactive whiteboard or visualiser, you could then project the story with the words containing the target sound highlighted or underlined. Re-read the story together and ask the learners to highlight or underline those words on their copy of the story. If you are working without this technology, re-read the story and stop as you come to the words that they have identified and ask them to highlight or underline them on their own copy.

4. Ask the learners to complete a chart, which records the words that they have highlighted and identifies the spelling of the target sound in each word. For example, in the first story in Level 1:

## Jane and Jake

| Word | Spelling |
|------|----------|
| Jane | a-e |
| train | ai |
| late | a-e |

There are two charts on the following pages: one for Level 1 stories and one for Level 2 stories, which have more occurrences of the target sound.

# Sound Search

| Word | Spelling |
|------|----------|
|      |          |
|      |          |
|      |          |
|      |          |
|      |          |
|      |          |
|      |          |
|      |          |
|      |          |
|      |          |
|      |          |
|      |          |
|      |          |
|      |          |
|      |          |
|      |          |
|      |          |
|      |          |
|      |          |
|      |          |
|      |          |
|      |          |
|      |          |

# Sound Search

| Word | Spelling |
|------|----------|
|      |          |
|      |          |
|      |          |
|      |          |
|      |          |
|      |          |
|      |          |
|      |          |
|      |          |
|      |          |
|      |          |
|      |          |
|      |          |
|      |          |
|      |          |
|      |          |
|      |          |
|      |          |
|      |          |
|      |          |
|      |          |
|      |          |
|      |          |
|      |          |
|      |          |
|      |          |
|      |          |
|      |          |
|      |          |
|      |          |
|      |          |
|      |          |
|      |          |